W9-CMZ-849

Glen Burnie H. S. Media Center

DIGITAL CAREER BUILDING™

Glen Burnie H. S. Media Center

CAREER BUILDING THROUGH

FAN FICTION WRITING

NEW WORK BASED ON FAVORITE FICTION

MIRIAM SEGALL

http://www.

FORUM

GLEN BURNIE HIGH

808.3 SEG

10332272139

Segall, Miriam
Career building through fan . . .

ROSEN
PUBLISHING®

New York

Published in 2008 by The Rosen Publishing Group, Inc.
29 East 21st Street, New York, NY 10010

Copyright © 2008 by The Rosen Publishing Group, Inc.

First Edition

All rights reserved. No part of this book may be reproduced in any form without permission in writing from the publisher, except by a reviewer.

Library of Congress Cataloging-in-Publication Data

Segall, Miriam.
Career building through fan fiction writing : new work based on favorite fiction / Miriam Segall. — 1st ed.
    p. cm. — (Digital career building)
Includes bibliographical references.
ISBN-13: 978-1-4042-1356-2 (library binding)
1. Fan fiction—Authorship. 2. Fan fiction—History and criticism. I. Title.
PN3377.5.F33W45 2007
808.3—dc22

2007029656

Manufactured in the China

CONTENTS

CHAPTER ONE

AN OVERVIEW OF FAN FICTION

The urge to tell a story is almost as old as time. Imagine yourself sitting around in a circle with a group of other people, listening to someone tell a tale full of adventure and wonder. You are then inspired to tell the same story to somebody else. He or she does the same and, as a result, the story is passed on from generation to generation. Over the years, technology advances, and the story is committed to the printed word and is shared more easily through technology. In essence, this story has outlived anyone who has ever told it.

Part of the storytelling tradition includes adding to a story that already exists. So what if someone is

Harry Potter fans, dressed in costume, pose with their copies of *Harry Potter and the Half-Blood Prince*, the sixth volume in the series.

 Passionate and enthusiastic fans care deeply about what happens on television shows such as *Grey's Anatomy*, a medical drama that airs on ABC.

enthusiastic and creative and wants to tell stories in a familiar setting? That is where fan fiction comes in.

Before we talk about fan fiction, it's important to define what it means to be a "fan." A fan may watch a television show on a regular basis and discuss it endlessly at school the next day. Many fans seek out other fans in real life and online. Some go to conventions and join clubs, and others go even further—sometimes dressing up like their favorite characters. When you are this serious a fan, you are engaging in the community rules of what's known as fandom.

Fans are passionate and enthusiastic. They care deeply about what happens next on *Lost* or *Grey's Anatomy*

FAN FICTION WRITING:

New Work Based on Favorite Fiction

Fans of *Lost*, a weekly television drama on ABC, are so devoted to the show that creating fan fiction means the fun never has to end.

or in the Harry Potter books, and they feel a sense of pride in becoming part of the created world. A TV show has only a certain number of episodes, and books and movies eventually end. But for fans, the fun doesn't have to end. They can keep imagining new endings, continuations, or entirely new stories. And so, fan fiction is born.

So What Is Fan Fiction?

Wikipedia defines fan fiction as "a broadly-defined term for fiction about characters or settings written by fans of the original work, rather than by the original creators." But another way to describe fan fiction (sometimes abbreviated as "fan fic") is that it takes a story created by someone—in the form of a book, television program, or movie—and uses it as a jumping-off point for new fiction within that world. It is important to distinguish between original fiction and fan fiction. Fan fiction is a channel for creative writing within a setting already defined by someone else, a way to share ideas with other fans, and a means to explore facets of popular characters that the fan may feel have been underdeveloped. It can also be a good way for fans to connect with other fans.

Although the definition of fan fiction seems fairly clear, it can get complicated because of one branch of the publishing world that creates books based on television shows, movies, and video games. Books that are direct adaptations of these types of entertainment are called tie-ins. Books that spin off entirely original ideas set in the world of the TV show or movie or video game are known as novelizations. The difference between these two categories and fan fiction is that tie-ins and novelizations are licensed by the people who own the TV show or movie to the publishing company. They hire a writer specifically for the project. People who write fan fiction are very rarely paid to do so. They write for their own enjoyment and the enjoyment of fellow fans. But while the monetary benefits of fan fiction writing are few, the creative possibilities are endless.

Types of Fan Fiction

Learning about fan fiction means learning a great deal of new words and terms—it's a lot like learning a whole new language! We'll start with the types of fan fiction that have been developed and exist today.

There are three general distinctions of fan fiction based on the length of the piece: Chaptered "fic" is written in a manner similar to traditional stories told in serials (think of a favorite television show with cliffhanger endings at the end of each episode). In other words, each chapter is released separately as it is finished. That way fans can enjoy the story a bit at a time.

Single-chapter stories of any length are usually referred to as one-shots because they will not be continued. You can also think of them as standalone stories. Some fan fiction stories are very short. One type, called a drabble, is traditionally a story exactly 100 words in length. This is a fun and challenging type of fan fiction.

Fan fiction writers have come up with other types as well:

- Story fiction—This type of fan fiction is a continuous story that lasts a few posts or threads. The topics are open to any genre.
- Series fiction—The author creates a spin-off of his or her own (for instance, *Degrassi: The College Years*) and posts a new episode regularly.
- Episode fiction—In this type of fan fiction, the author makes up his/her own episode for future seasons.
- Character fiction—This is a type of fan fiction where the story revolves around one character and usually follows the character in his or her everyday life.
- Round robin—This is considered to be the most "interactive" type of fan fiction. Fan fic authors post a paragraph to a story and then let other authors

 Fan fiction as we know it today grew out of fan culture for *Star Trek*, which aired from 1966 to 1969.

post continuations, but in their own words and style. There can be some very entertaining results!

History of Fan Fiction

 (From "History of Fan Fiction" by Laura Hale)

- **1421** John Lydgate, one of the most famous authors of the fifteenth century, writes "The Siege of Thebes," a continuation of Chaucer's *The Canterbury Tales*.

- **1710** Considered by many to be the first copyright law, the Statute of Anne was the short title for "An

Some people are such rabid fans of *Star Trek* that they will go to fan conventions dressed in costume.

Act for the Encouragement of Learning, by vesting the Copies of Printed Books in the Authors or purchasers of such Copies, during the Times therein mentioned." It was named after Queen Anne of Britain, during whose reign it was enacted.

- **1790** First copyright law is put on the books in the United States. It was signed by George Washington on May 31.

- **1869–1930** Fans begin to rewrite, parody, revise, and draft alternate endings to the works of Lewis Carroll. Some of his more famous "fans" include authors Christina Rossetti, Frances Hodgson Burnett, and E. Nesbit.

- **1920–1930** Jane Austen fan fiction gains popularity.

- **1930** The Sherlock Holmes Literary Society is founded to promote the work of Sir Arthur Conan Doyle.

- **1967** *Spockanalia* is the first *Star Trek* fanzine. The original *Star Trek* series would be canceled in 1969.

- **1972** First *Star Trek* convention in New York.

- **1973** The term "Mary Sue" is coined by fan author Paula Smith in her parody "A Trekkie's Tale."

- **1975** *Man from U.N.C.L.E.* stories distributed by hand as "fannish" community is isolated and unorganized.

- **1976** *Star Trek: The New Voyages*, the first commercial compilation of fan fiction that had appeared in the *Star Trek* fanzines, is published by Bantam Books.

 Star Wars fans pose as their favorite characters at a fan convention held in Los Angeles in May 2007.

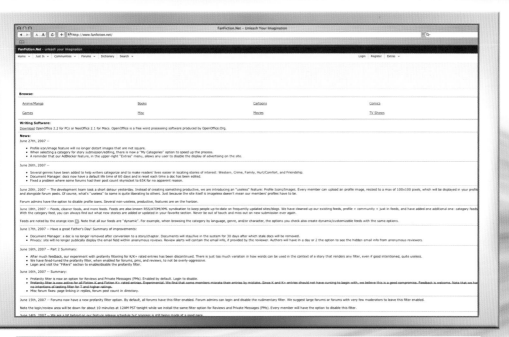

 FanFiction.net, the largest and most comprehensive Web site for fan fiction, launched in 1998.

- **1980** Usenet, one of first public, net-based gathering places for fans to post their writing and discuss fan fiction, is founded.

- **1981** The director of the Official Star Wars Fan Club sends *Star Wars* fanzines claiming they own all *Star Wars* characters and that zines may contain no pornographic material.

- **1992** The World Wide Web is "created."

- **1998** FanFiction.net goes online.

- **1999** LiveJournal, a popular blogging software, is founded.

- **1999** "Harry Potter and the Man of Unknown" by "Gypsy" becomes the first Harry Potter fan fiction posted to FanFiction.net. More than 15,000 Harry Potter stories have been posted since.

- **2005** Crackdown by the Motion Picture Association of America for copyright infringement.

Early fan fiction dates back to the seventeenth century, with unauthorized published sequels to such works as *Don Quixote* by Miguel de Cervantes. The instinct to continue a story past its ending later found fruit in "sequels" to books by Charles Dickens, Lewis Carroll, and Sir Arthur Conan Doyle.

Fan fiction as we know it today, however, became popular through the *Star Trek* fan base and fanzines published in the 1960s. The first *Star Trek* fanzine, *Spockanalia*, was published in 1967 and contained some fan fiction. Many of the early fanzines were produced by chapters of the Leonard Nimoy Association of Fans and included fan fiction based, not only on *Star Trek*, but on *Mission: Impossible*, in which Nimoy costarred for several years after *Star Trek* was canceled.

Fan fiction further spread in the 1970s and 1980s with the popularity of *Star Wars* and the *Star Trek* movies. Early Internet bulletin board and message groups such as USENET began to allow for easy posting of fan fiction. But when the World Wide Web became more prominent in the mid-1990s, the fan fiction landscape as we know it today was born. Many archives were created hosting specific sorts of stories, or stories for specific fandoms, and in 1998, FanFiction.net was created.

AN OVERVIEW OF FAN FICTION

 The most comprehensive fan fiction site available on the Internet, FanFiction.net became popular by giving fans the ability to self-publish fan fiction at one easy-to-reach Web site and the ability to review the stories. It now hosts millions of stories in dozens of languages and is the largest, most extensive, and most popular fan fiction online archive. In its wake, other fan fiction sites have begun to show up on the Web, some seriously devoted to maintaining an archive for fan fiction. Others offer a creative outlet for writers who want to parody their favorite work or offer reviews to other authors.

So what else do you need to know about fan fiction? What are the most popular topics? What rules must be followed? Let's take a look at the state of the field of fan fiction writing and get some insight!

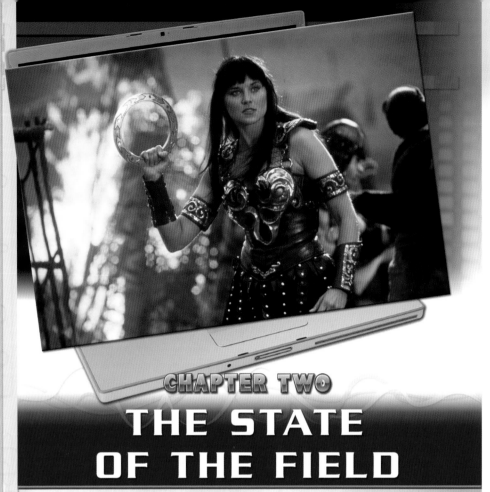

CHAPTER TWO

THE STATE OF THE FIELD

Fan fiction can develop from a television series, movie, or book. The Internet serves to boost the popularity of such entertainment, some generating more buzz than others. For example, the television series *Buffy the Vampire Slayer* premiered on the WB network in 1997. Almost immediately, a fan base developed online that created fan fiction stories on a variety of Web sites. The same thing happened after the premiere of *Xena: Warrior Princess*, a cable TV show that was a spin-off of another myth-spoof TV show, *Hercules*. Xena, as played by Lucy Lawless, and her sidekick Gabrielle, played by actress Renee O'Connor, proved so popular among the quickly growing fan base that thousands of fan fiction stories popped up online.

Lucy Lawless starred as the title character of *Xena: Warrior Princess*, a television show that spawned many pieces of fan fiction.

History and classic literature have also generated a great deal of fan fiction. For example, Jane Austen's work—especially her iconic novel *Pride and Prejudice*—has inspired a great number of fans to weave Elizabeth, Mr. Darcy, and other beloved characters into stories that pick up their lives where Jane Austen left off. One author, a librarian in Rathdrum, Idaho, spent ten years posting her writings about Mr. Darcy online. Simon & Schuster paid her a $150,000 advance to publish the works as a three-novel trilogy under the pseudonym of Elizabeth Aston.

Other historical works have inspired would-be writers to pick up the fan fiction pen. Neither Phillipa Ashley nor Rosy Thornton had ever written a word of fiction when they switched on the BBC's classic drama *North and South*, based on a nineteenth-century novel by Elizabeth Gaskell, in November 2004. Both women joined other fans in raving about the series—and its hero, played by Richard Armitage —on the BBC Web site. Both women later began posting stories on the Web. Ashley had the original idea of placing a version of Gaskell's novel in the present day, *North and South 2005*. Thornton, following the example of several others who were already doing so, began to write a continuation of the *North and South* story in its original Victorian setting. She called her piece *Roses and Thorns*. Both women were overwhelmed by the warm and generous response that their writing received from readers. Both were encouraged to go on writing and eventually landed book deals with major publishing houses.

Harry Potter fan fiction is probably the most widely popular topic since the year 2000. There are now tens of

thousands of stories created from J. K. Rowling's imagined universe, to the point where there are dedicated Web sites (like www.harrypotterfanfiction.com), devoted solely to the presentation of fan fiction stories about Harry, Hermoine, Ron, Draco Malfoy and all the other characters. Because of the epic nature of the books, several talented fan fiction writers have written complete novels in the Harry Potter world. Some have used their Harry Potter–based adventures to get book deals of their own.

Chilean journalism student Francesca Solar wrote her first Harry Potter fan fiction story at the age of twenty-one. She began her writing career after she read J. K. Rowling's fifth Harry Potter book, *Harry Potter and the Order of the Phoenix*. She was disappointed by it and decided to write a sequel of her own. "The Decline of the High Elves" was read and reviewed by over 80,000 Harry Potter fans from around the world.

"When I read the fifth book, I was so disappointed. I'm a very critical reader, and I'm a huge fan, so the expectation of this fifth book was great," Solar said, according to the BBC. "I took the principal characters, and I did a story that is richer than Rowling's story, because you can have access to the thoughts and feelings of all of the characters. In the Harry Potter saga, you can only have access to Harry's feelings and thoughts. That is a partial view of the Potter universe."

Solar never expected her book to have such global appeal. She received letters from all over the world from fans telling her that they liked her book better than *Harry Potter and the Half-Blood Prince*.

BBC NEWS | Entertainment | Potter fanfic writer launches first book

http://news.bbc.co.uk/2/hi/entertainment/6245333.stm

Home | News | Sport | Radio | TV | Weather | Languages

Search

UK version | International version | About the versions

Low graphics | Accessibility help

BBC NEWS

The News in 2 minutes

News services
Your news when you want it

News Front Page

Last Updated: Thursday, 11 January 2007, 11:34 GMT

E-mail this to a friend   Printable version

Potter fanfic writer launches first book

Africa
Americas
Asia-Pacific
Europe
Middle East
South Asia
UK
Business
Health
Science/Nature
Technology
Entertainment
Also in the news

Video and Audio

Have Your Say
In Pictures
Country Profiles
Special Reports
RELATED BBC SITES
SPORT
WEATHER
ON THIS DAY
EDITORS' BLOG

The debut novel from a Chilean writer who shot to fame after writing her own "fanfic" version of JK Rowling's Harry Potter stories has been released.

La Septima M - The Seventh M - is the first of three books that 23-year-old Chilean journalism student Francisca Solar was contracted to write by publishers Random House, following the online success of her unofficial sixth Harry Potter story, Harry Potter and the Decline of the High Elves.

Launched at the recent Frankfurt Book Fair, La Septima M centres on a mysterious series of suicides amongst young people in the fictional community of Puerto Fake.

"All the things I know about literature, about writing, I learned in the fan fiction world," Solar told BBC World Service's The Word programme.

"I owe it everything."

Online smash

Solar began her writing career when she found she was so disappointed with JK Rowling's fifth Harry Potter book, Harry Potter and the Order of the Phoenix, that she wanted to write her own sequel to it.

The Decline of the High Elves became a massive online smash, generating 80,000 views and positive reviews from Harry Potter fans around the world.

"When I read the fifth book, I was so disappointed - I'm a very critical reader, and I'm a huge fan, so the expectation of this fifth book was great," Solar said.

"I took the principal characters and I did a story that is more rich than Rowling's story, because you can have access to the thoughts and feelings of all of the characters.

"In the Harry Potter saga, you can only have access to Harry's feelings and thoughts. That is a partial view of the Potter universe."

She admitted she had never expected the global response to her work.

"Many people from all around the world have written to me, from the US, from the UK, from Asia," she said.

"All these people wrote to me about the fanfic and said they liked it more than the official sixth book [Harry Potter and the Half-Blood Prince]."

However, the editors at Random House insisted they did not want "another JK Rowling" and wanted something fresh - hence La Septima M, which will itself be followed up by two further books to complete a trilogy.

Fan fictions - fanfics - are one of the staples of internet sites dedicated to popular books, films and TV shows. Depending on the type and writer, some generate a substatial number of readers, while others will attract only a handful of browsers.

Solar wrote her Harry Potter fanfic at the age of 21

BBC WORLD SERVICE
The Word
Questions and talk with the world's best writers

GETTY IMAGES

66 All these people wrote to me about the fanfic and said they liked it more than the official sixth book 99

› Reviews of Harry Potter and the Half-Blood Prince

Francesca Solar, a twenty-one-year-old Chilean journalism student, received a publishing contract on the basis of her Harry Potter fan fiction.

One particularly interested reader turned out to be an editor at Random House, who immediately signed up Solar to write original novels. *La Septima M* is the first of three books Solar was contracted to write about a mysterious series of suicides amongst young people in the fictional community of Puerto Fake. "All the things I know about literature, about writing, I learned in the fan fiction world," Solar told BBC News. "I owe it everything."

For the most part, the topics mentioned appeal primarily to women, and fan fiction writers are predominantly female. But let's not forget that modern fan fiction essentially began in the 1960s with *Star Trek*, and that the movie *Star Wars* heavily influenced would-be fan fiction writers. So why do so many women write fan fiction? By and large because it's a way for them to express themselves on topics they might not talk about in their day-to-day lives. Writing gives them freedom, even if some writers feel that people put fan fiction down as "derivative" or "low class." Wrote one fan fiction writer on her LiveJournal blog, "I still think that the fanfiction [sic] community is the most amazing women's art culture I've ever experienced, and quite possibly the most amazing there has ever been, just in terms of sheer numbers and output." Beyond being a creative outlet, fan fiction is an entire community that brings fans together.

Categories

When you write fan fiction, it is important to learn the terminology that goes along with it. There are rules that have been put in place by those who are experienced fan fiction writers. By learning the official rules and terms,

 World of Warcraft, a popular Internet-based video game, has spawned many works of fan fiction.

you can prepare yourself for what to expect when becoming a fan fiction writer.

First, when talking about fan fiction, we must start with the original published material, otherwise known as canon. Canon refers to the "official" source material upon which fan fiction can be based, such as a television show like *Buffy the Vampire Slayer*, books like the Harry Potter series, or even video games like *World of Warcraft*. When something is considered "canon" it is understood, at least in fan fiction terms, to be "fact." Details as complex as the laws of physics in a given story universe or as minute as how a character's name is meant to be spelled can be referred to as "canon" details. The source material

must specifically show these details, including character behavior.

Some fan fiction writers create their own rules, asking that other fan fiction writers follow them or "jump off" from them as well. So instead of using the canon for the original world, we end up with a "fanon" for an already-established fan fiction universe. An example of a common fanon concept would be one where Draco Malfoy, the teenage nemesis from the Harry Potter series, has a fondness for leather pants. This concept shows up in fan fiction frequently even though in the books, films, and games, he has neither worn nor stated a liking for leather pants.

This can also sometimes refer to a fact or term from the canon, which is often adopted by the fandom and subsequently repeated in fan fiction at a frequency not seen in the original material. For example, Australian Dr. Robert Chase from *House* was referred to as a "wombat" in only one episode, but the fact is played on constantly in *House* fan fiction. Similarly, Xander Harris, from *Buffy the Vampire Slayer*, often calls his friend Willow Rosenberg "Wills" in fan fiction, but never once on the series.

Many terms pop up relating "canon" to "fanon." First there is the crossover story, in which either characters from one story exist in (or are transported to) another pre-existing story's world, or more commonly, characters from two or more stories interact. Imagine characters from *CSI: Crime Scene Investigation* solving crimes in the world of Harry Potter, or Mr. Darcy from *Pride and Prejudice* time traveling to be part of *Desperate Housewives*. "Movieverse" refers to fan fiction based on movie adaptations of books.

 Almost as soon as the television show *Buffy the Vampire Slayer* (featuring David Boreanaz and Sarah Michelle Gellar, *above*) debuted on the Warner Brothers network in 1997, a thriving fan fiction culture began.

In other words, a fan fiction story idea may come specifically from the movie version, rather than the book.

Some fan fiction categories are very complex and require lots of planning and thought. Some fans go as far as to create a virtual season for a television show. This is usually a group effort to produce a collection of fan stories or scripts portraying episodes of an entire season of a television program. Most of the time it is one that has been canceled or is no longer producing new episodes. When a favorite television program gets canceled, the fun doesn't have to end!

Relationships

There is little more important in a fan fiction story than how characters interact with one another. In other words, fan fiction writers spend a lot of their time creating romances between characters, sometimes in surprising ways. Creating these relationships, which is known as 'shipping (short for relationship), creates distinct groups of fans who root for the relationship to continue, even if this has no bearing at all on what happens in the movie or on TV. A classic example of 'shipping happened with fans of *Buffy the Vampire Slayer*, where some fans were rabidly for Buffy and Angel to get together. Another group were keen on Buffy and Spike as a couple. Fights would break out online and sometimes there would be bad blood between the two groups. Fans are extremely vested in character relationships, especially with characters on a long-running TV show with many changes in casting and story. Another example of 'shipping is very apparent in the Harry Potter series. Many fans would like to see Ron and Hermione end up together, and other fans would like to see Harry and Hermione together.

Sometimes these pairings, as done in fan fiction, are more for humor's sake. Acid pairing means that these pairings take two (possibly more) characters that, under normal logic, would never be romantically involved. These are generally done in humor and parody fan fiction.

Even more controversial is the category known as real person fiction. This is fan fiction featuring and starring real people, usually celebrities. In general, the authors seem to adopt the public personas of the celebrities in question as their own characters, building a fictional universe based on the supposed real-life histories of their idols. Information from interviews, documentaries, music videos, and other publicity sources are assimilated into the "canon" on which the stories are based. The first known "RPF" is believed to have been authored by members of the Brontë family, who went on to become famous for writing the novels *Jane Eyre* (Charlotte) and *Wuthering Heights* (Emily). Based on a children's role-playing game about the Napoleonic Wars, the series featured the Duke of Wellington; his two sons, Charles and Arthur; and their archenemy, Alexander Percy, partly based on Napoleon. Over the years, Arthur evolved into an amazingly charismatic and powerful figure, the Duke of Zamorna. Percy became a tragic villain, partly inspired by John Milton's Satan from *Paradise Lost*. These stories were not published until well over a hundred years later, but as children, the Brontës used them to polish their writing skills. Eventually they became professional authors.

FAN FICTION WRITING:

New Work Based on Favorite Fiction

Special Terminology

The most popular, and perhaps notorious term associated with fan fiction is the "Mary Sue." Let's let Dr. Merlin's Guide to Fan Fiction (http://missy.reimer.com/library/guide.html) explain what a Mary Sue is:

"You already know Mary Sue. Mary Sue is the perky, bright, helpful sixteen-year-old ensign who beams about the ship. Everyone on the ship likes Mary Sue, because Mary Sue is good at everything. Mary Sue is an engineer, a doctor in training, a good leader, an excellent cook, and is usually a beautiful singer. Mary Sue often has mental powers that may manifest themselves as telepathy, precognition, or magic. Her past is tragic, more so than any other character on the series. Her name is often the author's name, be it a net.name, a favored nickname, or the author's middle name (this is seen in the most famous Mary Sue of all time, Wesley Crusher, who was named after *Trek* creator Eugene Wesley Roddenberry). By the end of the story, Mary Sue will . . . have beamed away amid cheers from all the regulars, or will be dead, usually accompanied by heavy mourning from the cast. The reader, on the other hand, will be celebrating."

Mary Sue is a very idealized version of the fan fiction author, too perfect for words and (at least according to many fan fiction readers) extremely annoying to read about. In other words, writing one's self into fan fiction is frowned upon by readers. Avoid the temptation of writing yourself into your fan fiction story.

Now, what if you want to write fan fiction but need something extra? That's where challenge fic comes in.

A game played within writing circles, challenge fic combines the concept of fan fiction with a contest format.

This is an informal game played in writing circles. One person says "Hey, I dare you to write about [X]!" and anyone who likes the idea responds with a story about it. [X] can be a character or characters, a crossover, a situation, an event, or even a set of funny lines or objects that must be included within the body of the story. A challenge must be interesting, unusual, and original. For example, if characters "X" and "Y" have been written as a couple a hundred times already, asking for more stories about them is not a challenge.

And sometimes, a story knows that it's a story. When characters start talking directly to the audience, it's known as breaking the fourth wall. If they reference other fan fiction, canon, or outside stories and know it, that's

Wil Wheaton starred on *Star Trek: The Next Generation* as Wesley Crusher, widely considered by fans as the most famous "Mary Sue" of all time in any medium.

called metafiction. And a greater step is when fan fiction starts criticizing itself or other fan fiction stories. Taking its cue from the parody television show *Mystery Science Theater 3000*, this term is called misting (or MSTing, using the acronym of *Mystery Science Theater*.)

Now we will look at how to create your own fan fiction and make it the best it can possibly be.

CHAPTER THREE

WRITING YOUR OWN FAN FICTION

Now you know what fan fiction is, how it got started, who's writing it, and what the key issues are. Are you ready to take your fan fiction writing talents to the next level? Here are a few tips that will help you in your quest to write not only the fan fiction of your choice, but good fan fiction.

If you haven't already started writing your own fan fiction, here are a few tips to get you started. Think of a movie, book, TV show, cartoon, or other source you would like to use characters from. It could be something that's no longer airing, like *Buffy the Vampire Slayer*, *The X-Files*, or *Star Trek*. It could be a current show like *Grey's Anatomy* or a movie like *Spider-Man*. Or it could be a

Above is a scene from top-rated medical drama *Grey's Anatomy*. The heavy concentration on romance has spurred many fans to create fan fiction spin-offs.

video game such as *World of Warcraft*, *Halo*, or *Quake*. There are lots of ideas to choose from!

Second, devise a plot and a setting, and any possible extra characters of your imagination that you might wish to add. Just keep in mind that extra characters do not always make a story better and are even frowned on in some communities because they add additional clutter to the story. You don't want to make things too complicated for yourself!

Jot down your plot somewhere so you don't forget what you're writing about. Create an outline or keep a list of ideas.

Once you're ready, begin to write your story in the most descriptive, attractive, and appealing way possible. Get your ideas out there on paper, and then go back and hone the details. Remember to go back and proofread after you have finished! You might want to search for a beta reader, which is someone who will look over your work for you to help improve it by pointing out your strengths and weaknesses as a writer.

QUICK TIP Don't forget to back up your work and save it on a portable hard disk, in your e-mail in-box, or anywhere that isn't your hard drive. You may even want to print out a copy of your story. The last thing you want is for something you worked so hard over to disappear!

When possible, publish your work. How can you do this? You can get a free membership to publish fan fiction on several available sites.

FAN FICTION WRITING:

New Work Based on Favorite Fiction

Freedom of speech is an important issue for fan fiction writers, who write unauthorized fiction based on already-created characters.

Where to publish your fan fiction: Look at fan Web sites for your favorite television programs, movies, and books. You may find links to specific fan fiction sites that way as well.

Submitting your work usually involves registration to create your own username and password, followed by signing an agreement to stick to the site's rules and conditions. Once you have done this, you can then upload your fan fiction writing using the Web site's server. Afterwards, the story will be made available on the Web site for everyone to see. There may also be the option of restricting it to be viewed by only your closest friends.

TECH TOOLS You can also set up your own Web site or blog. Many fan fiction writers publish their work on their own on sites hosted by www.blogger.com or LiveJournal, probably the most popular Web site for fan fiction. LiveJournal, especially, has very strong community links that allow for discussion and feedback.

The great thing about using a blog or posting your story on some of the Web sites mentioned is that your story will get feedback, sometimes hundreds of comments. Everyone has an opinion—and some of those opinions can be very loud indeed—but remember to judge criticism fairly so that you can apply it to your next attempt at fan fiction. Most of the time you can approve of comments before allowing them to post.

Those are the basics of getting your own fan fiction up and running. But it's very important to consider how to make your fan fiction the best it can be. How do you write in your own voice, be mindful of any copyright issues, and write in a manner that will appeal to readers?

- Write your story in chapters, with each chapter in a separate document for easier writing and editing. It is also handy when you publish your story because you have to publish each chapter separately.

- Try to write your story in a way that will appeal to your readers. If you are a beginning writer, don't worry. You'll get better the more you write.

- Most fan fiction has characters from one book, TV show, or movie, or from other possible sources. Trying to incorporate too many sources, however, may make things more complicated for you because it's hard enough to keep one story straight. Trying to juggle several may give both you and your readers a big headache.

- Don't let people pressure you into submitting a chapter before it's ready. Make sure you're happy with it before you submit. What you write represents you to other people, so you want your readers to see the best possible story.

- People hate inconsistencies and continuity errors. Make sure that your fiction is consistent with what is already known about the universe for which you are writing. You don't want to get angry e-mail that you broke a rule already set by the universe you're writing in.

- Remember, shorter is not always better. A longer, more developed chapter—or even a longer fic without chapters—can be much more satisfying than a short one.

- Fans love pairings. They might be more interested in your fic if you include a little bit of romance in it. You don't necessarily have to go overboard with it, but it definitely doesn't hurt to include some kind of romantic tension or relationship development.

- People might not like continuous spelling or grammar mistakes. Use spell-check or a beta reader before you submit because there's nothing like an e-mail from a reader pointing out your grammatical errors to make you feel bad.

- The summary is everything! If people see a summary like, "This is my first fic EVER. PLz Review. R&R," they might be turned off and not want to read your stories. A better summary is something written like this: "Cha.1 is experiencing strange dreams, and somehow, a mysterious girl is involved. [Pairing here (if there is one).]" Leave "what if" or suspense questions in your summary.

But wait, we're still not done! Here are more quick tips to writing fan fiction, according to "Wayne's This and That" (http://www.waynesthisandthat.com/tensteps.htm).

- Avoid starting a story with a long narrative passage: Readers are more interested in reading about action rather than relying on a narrator to tell them what's happening. It is a common mistake to start a story with a slow-moving narrative passage. If you avoid that mistake, you'll stand out as a better-than-average

 Wayne's This and That (http://www.waynesthisandthat.com) has hundreds of tips for the aspiring fan fiction writer.

author. Capture your readers' interest by starting with lively action! Or begin by showing a character doing something that is very typical of him or her.

- Show, don't tell: Don't just tell your readers that something is beautiful. Show them why it is beautiful and allow them to discover its beauty for themselves. Show the reactions the beauty inspires in your characters. This adds life and movement to the scene.

- Avoid repetition: Repetition turns up in many different forms, all of them bad. Don't use the same word twice in the same sentence. This applies to prefixes and suffixes too. Don't place sentences that are the same length next to each other. Don't use two phrases to describe the same thing (like a person staggering and stumbling).

- Avoid clichés: Clichés are commonly used phrases like "raining cats and dogs." Clichés can also show up in characters such as "the absent-minded professor" or in plots, for example, when the cavalry rides to the rescue at the last moment.

- Avoid qualifiers: Adverbs help clarify verbs but they also weaken their impact. A better solution is to find a more descriptive verb that shows the reader what you want him or her to see. If you just can't find the right word, use your dictionary or thesaurus.

- Keep modifiers close to the word they modify: Consider the following sentence: "The cat walked around the potted geranium with bushy ears." This example makes it sound like the geranium has bushy ears. It reads more clearly as: "The cat with bushy ears walked around the potted geranium." Most of the time this mistake is more subtle than the example but can still confuse the reader.

- Don't use "he/she said" if it's not needed: When only two people are talking, use "he said" and "she said" only a couple of times in the beginning of the dialog. Readers are smart enough to follow who's talking from then on.

- Use contractions in dialogue: That's how real people talk. It'll make your dialogues smoother and more realistic. Read the dialogue out loud and listen for inconsistencies. Is this how the characters talk?

- Cut out extraneous words: Most fan fiction fails to read smoothly because authors use more words to describe a scene than are needed. The result is that the story reads unevenly. This is also called over-writing. Imagine you have to pay for each word in your story and the ones that can be cut will stand out. Give words like "the," "and," "even," and "just" an extra hard look. Many times these can be dropped to make the passage sound more dynamic and active. Trust your readers to fill in the story using their imaginations.

- Conquer "-ly" confusion: What's the difference between the following two sentences:

He smells bad.
He smells badly.

The first sentence states that the man in question has a bad odor. The second says that there is something wrong with his nose and he isn't able to smell effectively. These examples demonstrate that the -ly suffix is used to convert an adjective into an adverb. Mastering this simple rule will help clarify what you are trying to say about a character.

- Rewrite: Always rewrite your story several times, preferably with a couple of weeks of break between each one, before posting it online. The key to good rewriting is to proofread slowly. Writers are so familiar with their work that sometimes when they look at it they don't really read but just skim it. Their memories fill in the words they jump over. The hazard is that this permits mistakes to be jumped over as well. Maintaining a list of mistakes you repeatedly make will help focus your attention on them during proofreading.

- Use a spell-checker: You work hard to draw your reader into the world of your story. A single misspelled word is like a slap in the face to readers. It shocks them out of the story by reminding them that it's just something they're reading. The same goes for awkward sentence structure. If your reader doesn't understand a sentence, he or she will have to go back and read it again to make sense of it. This is very distracting.

WATCH OUT

Disclaimers: One more very important issue: MAKE SURE YOU WRITE A DISCLAIMER IN YOUR STORY. A disclaimer is where you tell where you got your characters from. This is necessary to keep from being sued. Disclaimers are useless, however, if the author doesn't want people writing fan fiction on his or her works. It's rare, but it does happen. For example, Fanfiction.net has a list of people that don't want their characters in stories, such as authors like Robin

A typical disclaimer on a fan fiction site might read like this: "I am just borrowing [the characters] for this fan fiction and mean no disrespect, nor am I making a profit on the work."

Hobb and George R. R. Martin, and filmmakers like George Lucas. The last thing you want after posting your fan fiction story online is a letter in the mail from a lawyer saying you violated copyright and will have to pay money. If someone has said specifically that he or she doesn't want fan fiction of his or her stories, steer clear.

Any responsible site that archives fan fiction stories will have a general disclaimer on the main page and any index pages, stating that the stories were written for fun and are reproduced on the Web for the enjoyment of other fans, and that there is no commercial intent. This is preceded or followed by a copyright disclaimer stating, for general fan fic sites, that all characters and settings are the copyright property of their creators, or on specific sites stating to whom the rights belong.

In chapter four, after discussing the most important points you need to know about writing fan fiction on a regular basis, we'll also mention some important legal issues to consider as you're preparing your career as a fan fiction writer.

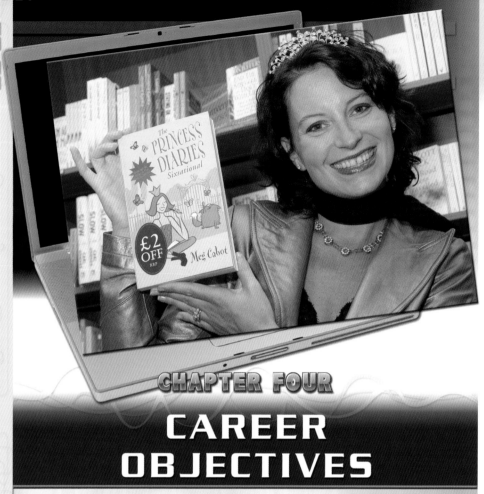

CAREER OBJECTIVES

You now know all the important fan fiction terms and have a step-by-step guideline for creating the fan fiction story of your dreams, but it's just as important to consider the following:

- Why write fan fiction?
- Who is the intended audience?
- Will the content, possible celebrity, or fifteen minutes of fame lead to unforeseen consequences on a personal and professional level?

So first, why focus on writing fan fiction? There are many reasons for teens to do so. It can be about expressing

Meg Cabot, best-selling author of *The Princess Diaries* and other books for young adults, got her writing start with fan fiction of Anne McCaffrey novels.

yourself or your personal beliefs, making a statement, or just having some fun. It can be to reach an audience of one person or of thousands, or to be part of a community of fellow writers and fans. Some teens use fan fiction as a way to learn the craft of writing, to explore all the ways of telling stories in a universe that's already defined for them, instead of having to make up something completely original. In time, some fan fiction writers may find that they are ready to create their own original work for others to build upon!

For some published authors, fan fiction was a way for them to find their writing style. Take Meg Cabot, author of *The Princess Diaries*, who told the *Wall Street Journal* in an article printed in September 2006 that she was once a fan fiction writer. She wrote stories inspired by Anne McCaffrey's fantasy novels about dragons when she was in high school and college. "I never told anyone. I've started admitting it now," she said, adding that she in turn was delighted to discover that her books had inspired hundreds of stories by fans.

Cabot is one of several authors, including fantasy writer Naomi Novik, who started a writing career in fan fiction. But even though she occasionally goes online to see the tally of fan fiction stories based on her work, she never reads them. Legal advisers warned that if she did read fan fiction, she'd be opening herself to potential lawsuits from fans who could claim she'd stolen their ideas.

Who is the intended audience? Depending on your goal of entertainment, enlightenment, social awareness, or any other objective, your target audience will change. Fan fiction that is meant to be funny or sweet will probably appeal more to younger readers, but the type of humor may also resonate with an older audience. More serious, saga-like fan fiction will appeal more readily to adults.

What is the ethical responsibility of a fan fiction writer? This is an important question because fan fiction is all about borrowing ideas that have been created by someone else. Even though copyright law is, so far, on the side of the fan fiction writer, there are many people who get very upset if the original work is copied in some way or another. Some have even gone so far as to try to sue or block fan fiction writers from posting their work online.

WATCH OUT **Legal issues:** In the legal world, fan fiction's status is somewhat unclear because of a lack of legal precedent in case law. Most legal scholars consider fan fiction to be a form of "derivative fiction." In the article "10 Big Myths About Copyright Explained," Brad Templeton states that fan fiction is a violation of copyright: "U.S. Copyright law is quite explicit that the making of what are called 'derivative works'—works based on or derived from another copyrighted work—is the exclusive province of the owner of the original work."

Several authors do not tolerate fan fiction or have policies regarding fiction derived from their work because of concerns about how characters are portrayed. For example, author Kristen Randle is deeply concerned about how fans portray her characters in any fan fiction derived from her books. She said the following in a private

Cathy Young, a political writer for *Reason* magazine, was involved in a nasty online skirmish after she published a piece extolling the virtues of fan fiction.

e-mail dated April 6, 2001, that is now posted on her Web site: "I do not wish anything that comes from me to be used in a way that I would judge to be outside my moral view."

Finally, will the content, possible celebrity, and/or fifteen minutes of fame lead to unforeseen consequences on a personal and professional level? It's a good question to ask because the vast majority of fan fiction writers do so under assumed names and seem to want to keep their anonymity. However, a few have achieved some degree of fame in the form of book deals (which was discussed in chapter two). But as we'll see in a couple of cases, revealing yourself as a fan fiction writer can prove both good and bad.

Take the case of Cathy Young. Known primarily as a writer for the political magazine *Reason*, she revealed in a piece in February 2007 that she was an avid practitioner of fan fiction. She ended up getting into an online skirmish with anti–fan fiction types that then spilled back over to her blog at *Reason*. Now, when most people Google Cathy Young, the first Web site that appears is the piece about fan fiction, and not anything relating to her day job. Even though she was proud to admit her hobby, Young may not have realized that on the Internet, perceptions might have changed. (For more information, check out Cathy's blog post at http://www.reason.com/news/show/118379.html.)

Then there is Cassandra Clare, who got her writing start in 2000 with a lengthy fan fiction piece based on Harry Potter. Her fame grew so widespread that she attracted fans of her own and was seen as something of

Cassandra Clare

biography   bibliography   links   news/events   journal   FAQ   home

Hi, I'm Cassandra Clare. I'm a writer from Brooklyn, New York. I am a huge fan of fantasy and gothic horror, and my first fantasy novel for young adults, *City of Bones*, was published this March by Simon and Schuster. The next book in the series, *City of Ashes*, will be released in March 2008 and the third, *City of Glass*, will come out in March, 2009. This website contains general information about me, my life, my work, and writing. If you want to know more about *City of Bones* and the *Mortal Instruments* trilogy, there's a website dedicated to the series—just click the picture frame below!

Good news addendum: I'm happy to report that City of Bones hit the *New York Times* bestseller list a few weeks after it came out! Yay!

July news update: I'm heading to London for my UK book launch on the 1st. I'll be blogging the launch from my Bebo page — and giving away free signed copies of City of Bones, along with other cool things like a video iPod. Come check it out!

Cassandra Clare's fan fiction proved so popular it attracted an online following and Clare became something of an Internet celebrity. Now she is a *New York Times* best-selling author of young-adult original fiction.

a rock star in the fan fiction world. But a year later, questions arose about her possible plagiarism of a fantasy novel by Pamela Dean, and Clare ended up being banned from Fanfiction.net. The debate was never fully resolved (even though Clare apologized for the possible error), and Clare's writing didn't suffer. In fact, her first original novel was published in March 2007 by Margaret K. McElderry books.

CHAPTER FIVE

FINDING SUCCESS IN THE FAN FICTION WORLD

As the first four chapters show, there are many avenues of success for those who intend to begin their careers, or just explore their interests, in writing fan fiction. But for every would-be success story, there are thousands whose quest for fame and fortune fall by the wayside, just as with any creative avenue. So how is an aspiring teen fan fiction writer able to get his or her name out there?

Strong content. Whatever the subject matter and the distribution source, fan fiction will live and die by the story, the writing, and the voice. If the story is good, funny, provocative, revealing, shocking, or insightful, then there will be an audience, however limited, for the

Strong content, a professional attitude, and a way with marketing are all important in finding success in the fan fiction world.

In 2006, HarperCollins sponsored Avon FanLit, a collaborative fiction effort between its published authors and amateur contributors. It proved so popular, the publisher repeated the contest in 2007.

fan fiction piece. And sometimes the audience out there can be so big it may surprise you. Remember that you have only a few lines to capture the attention of your readers.

A good example is a contest by Avon, the romance imprint of the publisher HarperCollins. In late 2006 it came up with the concept of "FanLit," which asked a number of professional romance writers to come up with a story starter idea that would then be continued by fans. The end result, which included an ending chapter by another professional romance writer, was published as an e-book and downloaded thousands of times. The experiment was so popular that HarperCollins tried it

A Successful Fan Fiction Writer: Hannah Jones

She writes about a group of young wizards attending the Hogwarts School. She has legions of readers, a Facebook group, an Italian fan club, and even a Polish translation. Her name is Hannah Jones, and she is twenty years old.

Jones, who has been writing fan fiction since she was eleven, turned to the world of Harry Potter in her freshman year at Barnard College when she and a friend began the Shoebox Project. The Potter prequel focuses on Harry's now deceased parents and their friends Remus and Sirus as teens finding themselves in high school during the 1970s.

And as a result of the Shoebox Project, Jones is now a published author. Her first print book, a collection of poetry called "Cinquefoil," was published by New Babel Books in 2006.

again in 2007. The FanLit contest allowed fans to try their hand at writing within a contained universe—something that might not have happened if they had to create a story completely from scratch.

A professional attitude can also help get your name out there. Even though writing is a solitary activity, meeting deadlines is a fundamental requirement. Let's say you're asked to contribute a piece of fan fiction as part of a challenge fic with a strict deadline. If you

Hard work and a professional attitude go a long way to creating fan fiction and sustaining a career and online presence.

miss it, the entire story will suffer and you might not be asked again to contribute. The same things might happen if your fan fiction gives you the opportunity to write something original for money. All the usual rules apply: follow directions, take criticism, and most of all, meet deadlines. (If you can't meet a deadline, give a reasonable explanation. If you do get an extension, be absolutely certain to meet that deadline.)

Viral marketing also helps writers become known. Should your fan fiction attract an audience, the chances are good that the initial readers will then tell other people and word-of-mouth will kick in accordingly. Blatant self-promotion on your part can help to spread the word, but ultimately, organic word-of-mouth is the best tool at a fan fiction writer's disposal. Be proud of the writing that you do. Don't be afraid to tell others about it.

And of course, a little luck and serendipity never hurt. Talent and hard work are always important, but all it takes is for the right person to discover your fan fiction at the right time for magic to happen, if that's what you want. And if all you want is to learn how to write well and apply the craft and tools to original writing in the future, then you, too, will be a big success in the world of fan fiction. Good luck!

GLOSSARY

acid pairing These pairings take two (possibly more) characters that, under normal logic, would never be romantically involved. Generally done in humour and parody fan fiction.

blog Short for weblog, it is a frequently updated Web site, often in journal format. Many fan fiction stories are published on blogs.

canon The "official" source material upon which fan fiction can be based.

challenge fic Fan fiction piece written by several authors that focuses on a central idea or challenge.

crossover When characters from one story exist in (or are transported to) another pre-existing story's world, or more commonly, when characters from two or more stories interact.

disclaimer A statement that says which of the characters and settings used in a story belong to a writer and which characters belong to somebody else.

fandom A collective term used to describe all fans and their activities. Science fiction fandom originated in the 1930s, when the first clubs were created.

fan fic Short for fan fiction.

fan fiction Fiction about characters or settings, written by fans of the original work, rather than by the original creators.

fanon Facts or situations, especially those that are used frequently in fan fiction so as to become seen by many as an extended part of the canon.

feedback Any comment from a reader, viewer, or listener to a fan fiction writer about his or her creative work.

Mary Sue The generic name for any new character (usually female) who is an ego-stroke for the writer: she's beautiful, has amazing skills/powers, gets into a love affair with an existing character, or (usually) all of the above.

movieverse Fan fiction based on movies of original works of fiction.

MSTing Commentaries on fan fiction stories, written in the style of the television show *Mystery Science Theater 3000*; also called misting.

original fiction Refers to wholly original works of fiction, for example, not based on any preexisting stories that were written by another author.

real person fiction Fiction written about real people such as actors, politicians, athletes, and musicians.

virtual season A collaborative effort to produce a compilation of fan stories or scripts portraying episodes of an entire season for a television program.

FOR MORE INFORMATION

The Association of Writers & Writing Programs
Mail Stop 1E3
George Mason University
Fairfax, VA 22030-4444
(703) 993-4301
Web site: http://www.awpwriter.org
E-mail: services@awpwriter.org
An organization that works to develop college creative
writing programs.

The Authors Guild
31 E. 32nd Street, 7th floor
New York, NY 10016
(212) 564-5363
Web site: http://www.authorsguild.org
E-mail: staff@authorsguild.org
An organization dedicated to the protection of the First
Amendment rights of authors.

Canadian Authors Association
Box 419
Campbellford, ON K0L 1L0
Canada
(705) 653-0323
Web site: http://www.canauthors.org
E-mail: admin@canauthors.org
The national writing organization of Canada, dedicated
to the support and development of the Canadian writing
community.

Society of Children's Book Writers and Illustrators
8271 Beverly Boulevard
Los Angeles, CA 90048
(323) 782-1010
Web site: http://www.scbwi.org
E-mail: scbwi@scbwi.org
An organization that allows authors to interact with each other and network with professionals in the publishing industry.

Web Sites

Due to the changing nature of Internet links, Rosen Publishing has developed an online list of Web sites related to the subject of this book. This site updated regularly. Please use this link to access the list:

http://www.rosenlinks.com/dcb/fafi

FOR FURTHER READING

Bacon-Smith, Camille. *Enterprising Women: Television Fandom and the Creation of Popular Myth*. Philadelphia, PA: University of Pennsylvania Press, 1992.

Beahm, George W. *Fact, Fiction and Folklore in Harry Potter's World: An Unofficial Guide*. Charlottesville, VA: Hampton Roads Publishing Company, 2005.

Beahm, George W. *Muggles and Magic: An Unofficial Guide to J.K. Rowling and the Harry Potter Phenomenon*. Charlottesville, VA: Hampton Roads Publishing Company, 2005.

Bury, Rhiannon. *Cyberspaces of Their Own: Female Fandoms Online*. Harrisburg, PA: Morehouse Publishing, 2005.

Fiske, John. "The Cultural Economy of Fandom." *The Adoring Audience*, Lewis, Lisa, ed. New York, NY: Routledge, 1991.

Grossberg, Lawrence. "Is There a Fan in the House?: The Affective Sensibility of Fandom." *The Adoring Audience*, Lewis, Lisa, ed. New York, NY: Routledge. 1991.

Harris, Cheryl, ed. *Theorizing Fandom: Fans, Subculture and Identity*. Cresskill, NJ: Hampton Press, 1998.

Hellekson, Karen, and Kristina Hesse. *Fan Fiction and Fan Fiction Communities on the Internet*. Jefferson, NC: McFarland & Company, 2006.

Hils, Matthew. *Fan Cultures*. New York, NY: Routledge, 2002.

Jenkins, Henry. *Convergence Culture: Where Old and New Media Collide*. New York: NY: New York University Press, 2006.

Jenkins, Henry. *Fans, Bloggers, and Gamers: Media Consumers in a Digital Age*. New York, NY: New York University Press, 2006.

Jenkins, Henry. *Textual Poachers: Television Fans and Participatory Culture*. New York, NY: Routledge, 1992.

Lewis, Lisa, ed. *The Adoring Audience: Fan Culture and Popular Media*. New York, NY: Routledge, 1992.

Miller, Ron. *The History of Science Fiction*. London, England: Franklin Watts, 2000

Pugh, Sheenah. *The Democratic Genre: Fan Fiction in a Literary Context*. Brigend, Wales: Seren, 2006.

BIBLIOGRAPHY

Aside from the books, Web sites, and other materials listed in the previous sections, the following resources were used in the preparation of this book:

Aulfrey, Penelope. "Petrarch's Apes: Originality, Plagiarism and Copyright Principles within Visual Culture." MIT Media-in-Transition Conference. October 8, 1999. Retrieved May 25, 2007 (http://media-intransition.mit.edu/articles/index_alfrey.html).

Bates, Patricia. "Internet Exposure Helps Authors Find Mainstream Success." The Biz Report. September 18, 2006. Retrieved April 11, 2007 (http://www.bizreport.com/2006/09/internet_exposure_helps_fan_fiction_authors_find_mainstream_success.html).

BBC World News. "Potter Fanfic Writer Launches First Book." January 11, 2007. Retrieved April 15, 2007 (http://news.bbc.co.uk/1/hi/entertainment/6245333.stm).

Cadwalladr, Carole. "Harry Potter and the Mystery of Academic Obsession." Guardian. August 6, 2006. Retrieved April 10, 2007 (http://observer.guardian.co.uk/review/story/0,,1837941,00.html).

"FanLib Brings Fan Fiction into the Mainstream, Launches New Website with Major Media and Publishing Partners." Yahoo.com press release. May 10, 2007. Retrieved May 25, 2007 (http://biz.yahoo.com/bw/070510/20070510005297.html?.v = 1).

Hale, Laura M. "History of Fan Fiction." Retrieved May 25, 2007 (http://www.trickster.org/symposium/symp173.htm).

Hobb, Robin. "Vampires of the Internet." Retrieved April 10, 2007 (http://www.robinhobb.com/rant.html).

Jurgensen, John. "Rewriting the Rules of Fan Fiction." *Wall Street Journal.* September 16, 2006. Retrieved April 10, 2007 (http://online.wsj.com/public/article/SB115836001321164886-GZsZGW_ngbeAjqwMADJDX2w0frg_20070916.html).

Lo, Malinda. "Fan Fiction Comes Out of the Closet." AfterEllen.com. January 4, 2006. Retrieved May 25, 2007 (http://www.afterellen.com/Print/2006/1/fanfiction.html).

Thornton, Rosy. "From Fanfic to Published Novels." Birmingham Words. September 22, 2006. Retrieved April 15, 2007 (http://www.birminghamwords.co.uk/index.php?option = com_content&task = view&id = 734&Itemid = 49).

Young, Cathy. "The Fan Fiction Phenomena." *Reason.* February 2007. Retrieved April 15, 2007 (http://www.reason.com/news/show/118379.html).

INDEX

A

acid pairing, 25

B

"breaking the fourth wall," 27
Brontë, Charlotte and Emily, 25
Buffy the Vampire Slayer, fan
    fiction and, 16, 21, 22, 24, 30

C

Cabot, Meg, 43
canon, definition of, 21
canon details, 21–22
challenge fic, 26–27
chaptered fic, 8
character fiction, 8
Clare, Cassandra, 46–48
classic literature, fan fiction
    and, 17
crossover story, 22

D

disclaimers, 39–41
drabble, 8

E

episode fiction, 81

F

fan, definition of, 5–6
fan fiction
    careers and, 43, 53

categories of, 22–25
definition of, 6–7
ethics and, 44–46
fame/success from, 42,
    46–48, 49–53
history of, 9–14
publishing, 31–33
reasons for writing, 42–44
relationships in, 24–25, 34–35
rules of, 20–22
subjects written about, 16–20
types of, 7–9
writing your own, 30–41
FanFiction.net, 13, 14, 15, 48
FanLit contest, 50–51
fanon, definition of, 22

H

Harry Potter, fan fiction and,
    14, 17–20, 21, 22, 24–25,
    46, 51
House, fan fiction and, 22

J

Jones, Hannah, 51

L

LiveJournal, 13, 20, 33

M

"Mary Sue," 11, 26
metafiction, 27–29

About the Author

Miriam Segall is a writer living in New York City. She, too, has dabbled in fan fiction but found that her gifts lie elsewhere.

Photo Credits

Cover (hat) © www.istockphoto.com/Bobbie Osborne, (*Star Trek*) © Ron Wurzer/Getty Images, (http) © www.istockphoto.com/ Jente Kasprowski, (forum) © www.istockphoto.com/Marco Rullkoetter; p. 4 © Paco Serinelli/Getty Images; p. 5 greysanato-myfans.net; p. 6 www.lost-tv.com/fansection; p. 9 © ArenaPal/ Topham/The Image Works; p. 10 © Ethan Miller/Getty Images; p. 12 © Gabriel Bouys/Getty Images; p. 13 www.fanfiction.net; pp. 16, 23 © Getty Images; p. 19 (foreground) news.bbc.co.uk/ 2/hi/entertainment/6245333.stm; p. 19 (background) © www. istockphoto.com/Alexander Hafemann; p. 21 www.worldofwarcraft. com/index.xml; p. 27 community.livejournal.com/fanfic100/ profile; p. 28 Paramount/Everett Collection; p. 30 Gale Adler/© ABC/ Courtesy Everett Collection; p. 32 www.fos-ff.net; p. 36 www. waynesthisandthat.com; p. 40 www.fanfiction.net/s/3493243/1/; p. 42 © Keith Mayhew/PHOTOlink/Newscom; p. 45 (top) www. reason.com/news/show/118379.html; p. 45 (bottom) © www. istockphoto.com/bulent ince; p. 47 cassandra-clare.com/index.html; p. 49 © www.istockphoto.com/fabphoto; p. 50 dearauthor.com/ wordpress/2006/11/28/avons-fan-lit-ready-for-publication; p. 52 © www.istockphoto.com/Chris Schmidt.

Designer: Nelson Sá; **Editor:** Bethany Bryan; **Photo Researcher:** Amy Feinberg

Glen Burnie H. S. Media Center